HANDY CRAFTS

HOLIDAY HANDIWORK

Gillian Souter

Gareth Stevens Publishing
A WORLD ALMANAC EDUCATION GROUP COMPANY

★ Before You Start ★

Some of these projects can get messy, so make sure your work area is covered with newspaper. For projects that need paint, you can use acrylic paint, poster paint, or any other kind of paint that is labeled nontoxic. Ask an adult to help you find paints that are safe to use. You will also need an adult's help to make some of the projects, especially when you have to stitch fabric, poke holes with pointed objects, or use a craft knife or any other sharp cutting utensils.

Please visit our web site at: www.garethstevens.com
For a free color catalog describing Gareth Stevens Publishing's
list of high-quality books and multimedia programs,
call 1-800-542-2595 or fax your request to (414) 332-3567.

Library of Congress Cataloging-in-Publication Data

Souter, Gillian.
　　Holiday handiwork / by Gillian Souter.
　　　　p. cm. — (Handy crafts)
　　Includes bibliographical references and index.
　　Summary: Provides instructions for creating an assortment of craft items for such holidays as Valentine's Day, Easter, Halloween, Thanksgiving, and Hanukkah.
　　ISBN 0-8368-3050-4 (lib. bdg.)
　　1. Holiday decorations—Juvenile literature.　2. Handicraft—Juvenile literature.　[1. Holiday decorations.
　2. Handicraft.]　I. Title.　II. Series.
TT900.H6S68　　2002
745.594'16—dc21　　　　　　　　　　　　　　　　　　　　　　　　2001055086

This edition first published in 2002 by
Gareth Stevens Publishing
A World Almanac Education Group Company
330 West Olive Street, Suite 100
Milwaukee, Wisconsin 53212 USA

This U.S. edition © 2002 by Gareth Stevens, Inc. Original edition published as *Festive Fun* in 2001 by Off the Shelf Publishing, 32 Thomas Street, Lewisham NSW 2049, Australia. Projects, text, and layout © 2001 by Off the Shelf Publishing. Additional end matter © 2002 by Gareth Stevens, Inc.

Illustrations: Clare Watson
Photographs: Andre Martin
Cover design: Joel Bucaro and Scott M. Krall
Gareth Stevens editor: JoAnn Early Macken

Printed in the United States of America

1 2 3 4 5 6 7 8 9 06 05 04 03 02

Contents

Let's Celebrate!. 4

New Year Noises 6

Dancing Dragon 8

Be My Valentine. 10

Paper-and-Pin Hearts. 12

Passover Pocket 14

Speckled Eggs. 16

Chicks-in-a-Nest 18

April Fool!. 20

Flower Power. 22

Pumpkin Head. 24

Spider-on-a-String 26

Spooky Shades 28

Turkey Tubes 30

Nature Stamps. 32

Clay Dreidel 34

Star Bright 36

Sweet Wreath. 38

Dear Reindeer 40

Tree Baubles 42

Super Santa 44

Kwanzaa Beads 46

Glossary 48

More Craft Books. 48

Index 48

Let's Celebrate!

Holidays are special, festive occasions celebrated all around the world and all through the year!

Chinese New Year is celebrated a little later than our calendar New Year.

Welcome in the New Year with lots of noise!

Show people you love that you're thinking about them on Valentine's Day.

During Passover, Jewish people celebrate the idea of freedom.

Easter is a springtime holiday to celebrate new beginnings.

April Fool's Day is the perfect time for fun and harmless practical jokes.

4

In the northern half of the world, May Day is a spring or summer holiday.

Scary bats and black cats are some of the spooky things that appear on Halloween!

Thanksgiving and other harvest festivals celebrate the world of nature.

The Jewish holiday of Hanukkah is known as the "Holiday of Lights."

People of African descent celebrate Kwanzaa, a holiday of family, community, and culture.

People all over the world celebrate Christmas.

New Year Noises

Welcome the New Year with a ringing, rattling reception!

You Will Need

- 10 small bells
- 5 pipe cleaners
- pencil
- tape
- 2 paper or plastic cups
- rice
- markers

1 To make a bell shaker, thread a small bell onto each end of a pipe cleaner. Bend the ends to hold the bells in place. Add bells to four more pipe cleaners.

2 Bend the pipe cleaners in half. Arrange them around one end of a pencil.

3 Wrap tape tightly around the pipe cleaners to hold them in place on the pencil.

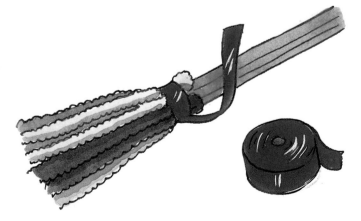

4 To make a cup shaker, put a few spoonfuls of dry rice in a paper or plastic cup.

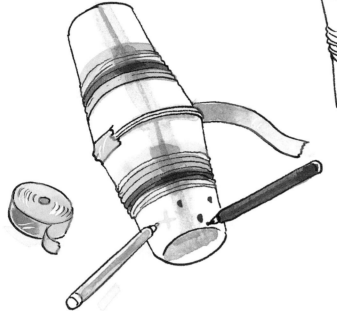

5 Tape another cup on top, with the open ends of the cups together. Decorate the shaker with markers.

★ Bright Idea ★
Make enough noisemakers for your whole family to join in!

7

Dancing Dragon

You Will Need

- scissors
- egg carton
- glue
- paint
- paintbrush
- cardboard tubes
- crepe paper
- tape
- felt or other fabric
- 2 pencils or small dowels

This sensational serpent will bob and sway its way through a Chinese New Year celebration!

1 Cut an egg carton in half. From one half, cut off two cups to make eyes and glue them on top of the other half.

2 Paint the egg carton with the eyes on top, inside and out, to make a dragon head. Also paint several cardboard tubes.

3 Cut strips of crepe paper to make streamers. Wrap tape around the middle of a bunch of streamers and stick them inside a cardboard tube. Repeat this step for each tube.

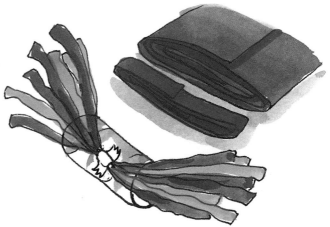

4 Make another bunch of streamers and tape it onto the head, behind the eyes.

5 Glue the head and the tubes onto a strip of felt or some other fabric.

6 Use the point of a scissors to poke a hole in the bottom of the head and in the bottom of the last tube. Push a pencil or a dowel into each hole.

★ **Bright Idea** ★
Hold the sticks high above you and make your dragon dance!

Be My Valentine

Send a sparkly pop-up greeting to someone special!

1 Draw an 8-inch by 4-inch (20-centimeter by 10-cm) rectangle on a piece of thin cardboard. Cut it out and fold it in half to make a square card.

2 Trace the heart pattern (above, right). Cut out the tracing and draw around it on another piece of thin cardboard. Cut out this heart and decorate one side of it with glitter glue.

10

3 Cut a strip of cardboard that is 4 inches by 3/4 inch (10 cm by 2 cm). Fold the strip in half, then make another fold 3/4 inch (2 cm) from each end (as shown).

4 Glue this strip onto the back of the heart (as shown).

5 Lay the heart, facedown, inside the square card. Put glue on each of the end tabs. Turn down the bottom tab, then close the card and press. When you open the card, the heart should pop up.

★ Helpful Hint ★
Write your Valentine's name on the front of the card before you deliver it!

Paper-and-Pin Hearts

Hang these hearts around your house or hand them to your sweetheart!

1 Fold a piece of white paper in half. Draw half of a heart along the fold.

2 Leave the paper folded and cut out the half heart with pinking shears or scissors that have a fancy edge.

3 Wrap tape around one end of a large needle to make a handle. Lay the heart on a piece of scrap cardboard. Use the needle to poke a pattern into the paper heart.

4 Lightly glue the heart onto colored cardboard. Cut the cardboard neatly around the heart, leaving room for a hole at the top.

5 Punch a hole at the top of the heart and thread narrow ribbon through it. Tie a bow or a knot in the ribbon to make a hanging loop.

★ **Bright Idea** ★
Make different paper-and-pin shapes for other festive occasions!

Passover Pocket

At Jewish Passover, someone hides
a piece of matzo bread called the
afikomen, and everyone searches for it.
Make an afikomen pouch to hide.

You Will Need
- ruler
- scissors
- felt
- straight pins
- needle and thread
- sequins
- glue

1 Measure and cut out a rectangle of
colored felt that is 11 1/2 inches by
4 inches (29 cm by 10 cm).

2 Fold over 4 inches (10 cm)
at one end of the felt. Pin the
two layers together at each side.

3 Thread a needle and sew along one edge of the folded section with neat stitches. Tie off the thread, then sew along the other edge.

4 Trim the two corners of the unsewn flap into gentle curves.

5 Arrange sequins on the flap and glue each sequin in place.

★ Bright Idea ★
Instead of matzo bread, put a small treat inside this pretty pocket.

Speckled Eggs

Colored eggs will last for years if you blow the eggs out of their shells before painting them!

You Will Need
- eggs
- pin
- metal skewer
- empty bowl
- bowl of water
- paper towels
- acrylic paints
- paintbrush
- sponge
- clear varnish

1 Make a hole in both the top and the bottom of an egg with a pin. Carefully poke a metal skewer through the holes to make them larger and to break up the egg yolk.

2 Gently blow the contents of the egg into a bowl. Be sure to get all the egg out, or it will smell terrible after a while. If you have trouble getting the contents out, make the holes a little bigger.

3 Rinse out the egg by holding it underwater and then blowing through it again. Drain the rinsed-out egg on paper towels.

4 Paint half of the egg with acrylic paint. When it is dry, paint the other half.

5 Dip the corner of a sponge into a different color of paint. Dab the paint onto the egg. When it is dry, brush on a coat of varnish.

★ **Bright Idea** ★
Dab on gold paint
for a dazzling effect!

Chicks-in-a-Nest

**Brighten up Easter and springtime
with this flock of fuzzy yellow peepers!**

You Will Need

- yellow food coloring
- glass of water
- cotton balls
- tweezers
- old newspaper
- scissors
- orange pipe cleaners
- glue
- beads or markers
- egg carton
- crepe or tissue paper

1 Add five or six drops of yellow food coloring to a quarter glass of water. Drop in a cotton ball, then lift it out with tweezers. If it is not bright enough, add more food coloring.

2 Color each cotton ball, one at a time. You will need two cotton balls for each chick. Place the cotton balls on folded newspaper to dry overnight.

3 When the cotton balls are dry, gently pull them back into shape. Cut small pieces of pipe cleaners and bend them into beaks. Glue the beaks onto the heads.

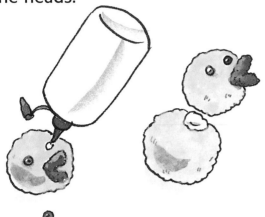

4 Glue on small beads for eyes or draw on eyes with a marker. Glue a head onto each body.

5 Use the lid of an egg carton to make a nest. Line the lid with strips of crepe paper or tissue paper. Arrange the chicks in their nest.

★ **Bright Idea** ★
Use the chicks alone in the nest or arrange both chicks and speckled eggs in it.

April Fool!

On April 1st,
wind up a jumping jack
and spring it on a friend!

1 Cut a piece of a drinking straw
so the bend is in the middle.
If you don't have bendable straws,
roll a square of paper tightly and
glue it down the edge. Then bend
it in the middle. You will need two
pieces of straw or two paper rolls
for each jumping jack.

2 Lay two straws or paper rolls
together, side by side. Wrap
a rubber band loosely around
them in the middle.

3 To wind up the jumping jack, hold one straw or paper roll and turn the other one as many times as possible.

4 Place the jumping jack in a small box without letting it unwind. Close the lid carefully, then open the box to make sure the jack jumps out. Rewind the jumping jack and pack the box again. Tie a ribbon around the box this time.

★ **Bright Idea** ★
Offer the box to a friend and watch what happens!

Flower Power

**Make a frilly fabric flower
to wear on May Day!**

1 Lay the lid of a jar on a piece of fabric. Draw around it with a pencil.

2 Cut out the circle with pinking shears. You will need to cut out three circles for each flower.

3 Thread a needle with doubled thread and tie a knot in the end. Sew a ring of stitches around each fabric circle (as shown).

4 Pull on the ends of the thread to gather the fabric into a petal. Knot the thread to hold the shape.

5 Sew together three gathered petal sections to make a full flower.

★ Bright Idea ★
Make these ruffly flowers in several bright colors. Then sew them onto a hat or a headband.

Pumpkin Head

A scary jack-o'-lantern face makes a great mask for Halloween!

You Will Need
- paper plate
- pencil
- markers
- newspaper or cardboard
- compass
- string
- scissors

1 Hold a paper plate up to your face. Position two fingers on the plate over your eyes and ask a friend to mark eye holes on the plate with a pencil.

2 Draw a pumpkin shape on the plate. Then draw in a jack-o'-lantern face.

3 Color the pumpkin face with markers.

4 Lay the mask on newspaper or cardboard. Poke eye holes into it with the point of a compass. Also poke a hole on each side of the face.

5 Tie a piece of string through one of the side holes. Try on the mask to check the fit before you tie the string through the other side hole.

★ **Bright Idea** ★
Wear your mask for trick or treat!

Spider-on-a-String

You Will Need

- scissors
- egg carton
- metal skewer
- paint
- paintbrush
- pipe cleaners
- tape
- elastic string

Here's a really creepy-crawly way to decorate for Halloween!

1 Cut off a single cup from an egg carton. With a metal skewer, carefully punch one hole in the top of the cup and eight holes around the sides.

2 Paint the outside of the cup and let it dry. Cut eight equal pieces of pipe cleaners for the legs.

3 Poke the legs into the eight side holes and bend them into shape.

4 Inside the cup, bend over the ends of the pipe cleaners and tape them in place.

5 Tie a knot in one end of some elastic string. Thread the other end of the string up through the hole in the top of the egg cup.

★ **Bright Idea** ★
Hang your spider somewhere spooky and watch it wiggle!

27

Spooky Shades

Shadowy candle shades cast an eerie glow on a Halloween night!

You Will Need

- clean plastic bottle
- craft knife
- scissors
- powder paint
- water
- paintbrush
- paper or thin cardboard
- black marker
- black paper or thin cardboard
- glue
- small candle
- glass jar

1   To make a clear plastic tube, ask an adult to cut both ends off of a plastic bottle by making a slit in the side of the bottle with a craft knife, then using scissors to cut all the way around.

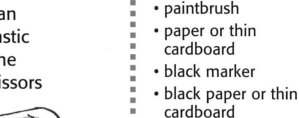

2   Mix powder paint with water. Paint the inside of the tube with a thin coat of paint and let it dry.

3   Draw bats, cats, and other Halloween shapes on paper or thin cardboard. Color them in with a black marker, then cut out the shapes.

28

4 Cut two strips of black paper or thin cardboard. Glue the strips around the top and bottom of the tube.

5 Glue the black Halloween shapes to the inside of the tube. Place a small candle in a clean glass jar and put your spooky shade over it.

★ Helpful Hint ★
Always ask an adult to light the candle and replace the shade when the candle is lit.

Turkey Tubes

Trace your fingers to form the feathers for these funny fowl napkin friends!

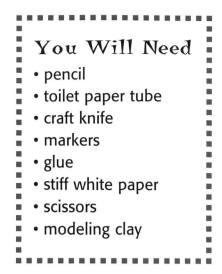

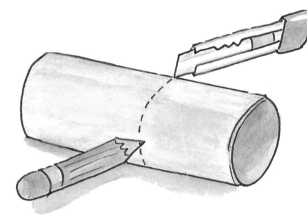

1 Draw a line around the outside of a toilet paper tube. Make the line closer to one end of the tube than the other. Ask an adult to cut along the line with a craft knife.

2 Color the two pieces of tube with a brown marker. Glue the tubes together (as shown) to make the turkey's head and body.

3 Place your left hand flat on a piece of white paper and draw around it. Repeat this step with your right hand. Color both hands with markers.

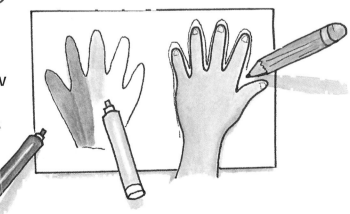

30

4 On white paper, draw two eyes, a beak, two feet, and a wattle (the red flap of skin on a turkey's neck). Color all of the turkey parts with markers.

5 Cut out the hands and glue them onto the back of the body tube to make a tail. Cut out the other turkey parts and glue them in place.

6 Stick a piece of modeling clay at the back of the tail (as shown) so the turkey will stand up.

★ **Bright Idea** ★
Roll up a napkin and slide it through the body tube to dress up your table for Thanksgiving guests!

Nature Stamps

Harvest some fruits and vegetables for a crop of festive fall designs that produce perfect pictures and wrapping paper — naturally.

You Will Need
- sharp knife
- fruits and vegetables
- towel
- powder paints
- water
- paintbrush
- plastic lids
- paper

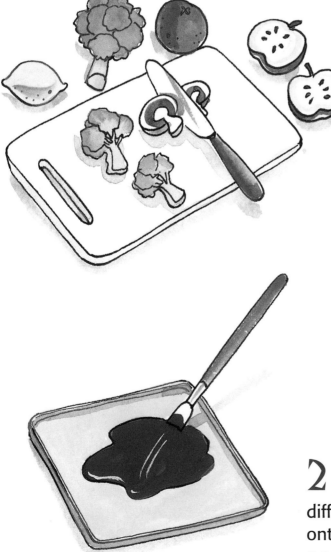

1 Ask an adult to cut all of the fruits and vegetables in half. Dry the cut sides with a towel.

2 Mix powder paint and water to a thick consistency. Mix up several different paint colors. Brush some paint onto the lid of a plastic container. Use a separate lid for each color of paint.

3 Press the cut side of a fruit or a vegetable into the paint. Wiggle it around, then press it firmly onto a sheet of paper.

4 Repeat step 3 to make as many prints as you want. Create a pattern of prints using different shapes and colors.

★ **Bright Idea** ★
Brush a thin coat of paint over the whole sheet of paper before you start printing.

Clay Dreidel

This traditional Hanukkah toy is a four-sided spinning top. See how many chocolate coins you can win playing the dreidel game!

You Will Need

- air-drying clay
- ruler
- blunt knife
- thin dowel
- fretsaw
- acrylic paint
- paintbrush
- metallic pen
- clear varnish

1   Knead a ball of clay until it is smooth. Roll it into a sausage shape, then flatten the sides with a ruler to make a long box shape.

2   With a blunt knife, cut one end of the clay into a **V** shape.

3   Turn the clay so the **V** shape is on its side. Carefully cut another **V** shape to form a point.

4 Make a straight cut across the clay for the top of the dreidel. Smooth all the corners with a damp finger.

5 Ask an adult to cut off a small piece of a dowel with a fretsaw. Push this piece of dowel into the top of the dreidel. Let the dreidel dry until the clay is hard.

6 Paint the clay with acrylic paint. When the paint is dry, draw symbols on each side of the dreidel with a metallic pen. Then, coat the dreidel with clear varnish.

★Helpful Hint★
Dreidels have Hebrew letters on each side for playing a traditional game. You can draw other symbols instead.

Star Bright

Make a shining Star of David for Hanukkah or Christmas.

1 Paint six ice cream sticks with yellow or gold paint. Let the paint dry.

2 Arrange three sticks in a triangle so each stick has one end resting on top of the end of another stick. Glue the ends together.

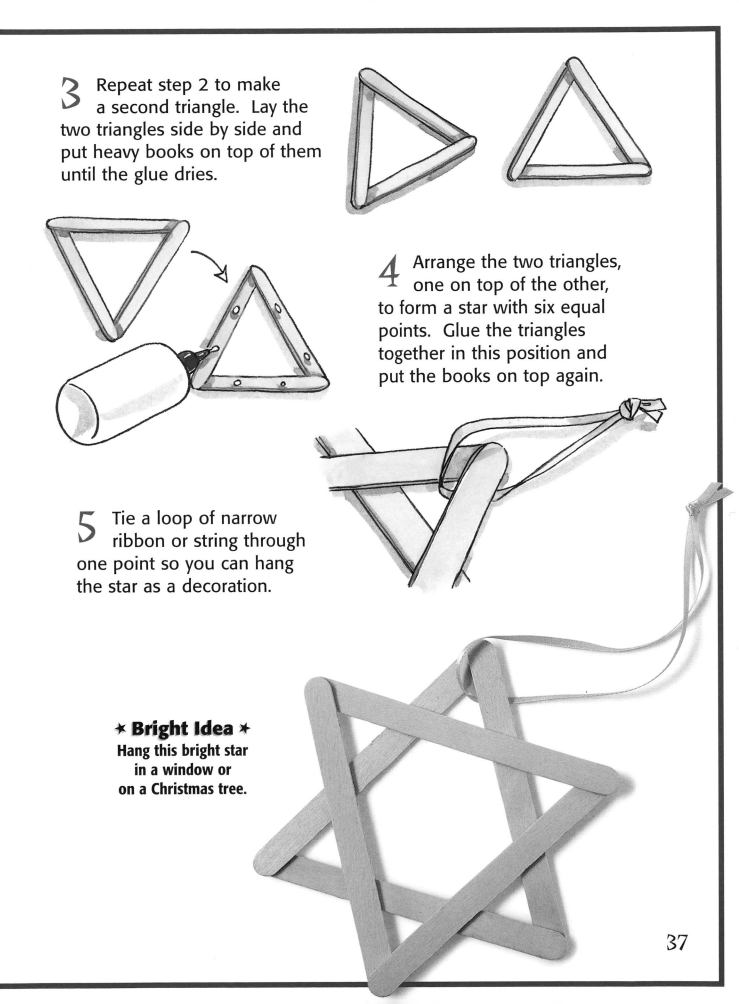

3 Repeat step 2 to make a second triangle. Lay the two triangles side by side and put heavy books on top of them until the glue dries.

4 Arrange the two triangles, one on top of the other, to form a star with six equal points. Glue the triangles together in this position and put the books on top again.

5 Tie a loop of narrow ribbon or string through one point so you can hang the star as a decoration.

★ Bright Idea ★
Hang this bright star in a window or on a Christmas tree.

37

Sweet Wreath

Decorate your door for Christmas with a wreath of candy treats!

1 Cut a large hole in the middle of a paper plate. Lay the cut plate over another plate and draw around the hole with a pencil. Cut the second plate along the pencil line.

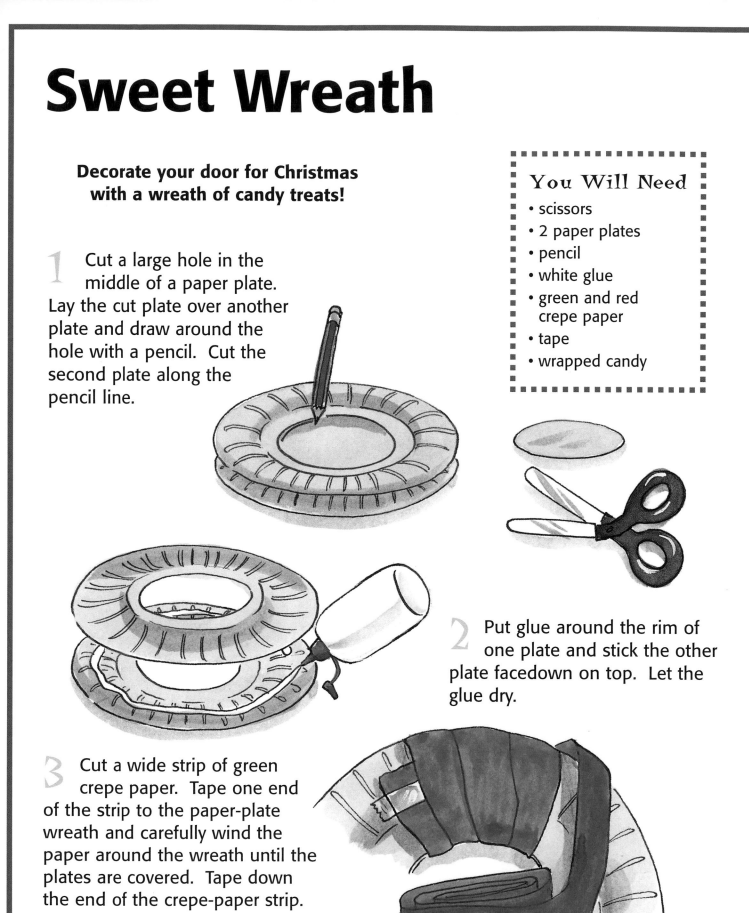

2 Put glue around the rim of one plate and stick the other plate facedown on top. Let the glue dry.

3 Cut a wide strip of green crepe paper. Tape one end of the strip to the paper-plate wreath and carefully wind the paper around the wreath until the plates are covered. Tape down the end of the crepe-paper strip.

4 Cut a narrow strip of red crepe paper and wind it around the wreath (as shown). Tape both ends at the back of the wreath.

5 Glue wrapped candy onto the front of the wreath and add a big crepe-paper bow.

★ **Helpful Hint** ★
Attach a loop of string to the back of the wreath, at the top, so you can hang it on a door or a wall.

Dear Reindeer

You Will Need

- pencil
- scrap paper
- scissors
- red felt
- marker
- stiff cardboard
- glue
- tape
- plastic headband
- ribbon

Wear these awesome antlers to show your Christmas spirit — or to play reindeer games!

1 Draw one antler shape on a piece of scrap paper by copying the picture on the next page. Cut out the shape.

2 Lay the antler cutout on red felt and trace around it with a marker. Cut out the felt shape. Repeat this step to make four felt antler shapes.

3 Cut two long strips of stiff cardboard. Bend each strip twice near the middle and glue the ends together (as shown).

4 Glue an antler shape onto each side of a cardboard strip.

5 Tape the two antler-covered strips onto a headband (as shown). Cover the headband by winding ribbon or a strip of felt around it. Glue the ends of the ribbon or felt strip in place.

★ **Bright Idea** ★
Wear your antler headgear to a holiday party!

Tree Baubles

These glittering, glimmering ornaments will make your Christmas tree sparkle!

You Will Need

- small jar
- thin white cardboard
- pencil
- scissors
- paper clips
- white glue
- heavy books
- tissue paper
- paintbrush
- clear varnish
- sequins and shiny candy wrappers
- narrow ribbon

1 Place a small jar on thin white cardboard and draw around it. Cut out two cardboard circles for each ornament.

2 Lay a paper clip on a cardboard circle so it sticks out over the edge. Glue another cardboard circle on top. Put some heavy books on the circles until the glue is dry.

3 Tear small squares of tissue paper. Glue them all over the ornament, folding them around the edges. When both sides are covered, brush on clear varnish.

4 Glue on sequins and scraps of shiny candy wrappers.

5 Thread a piece of narrow ribbon through the paper clip. Tie the ends to make a hanging loop.

★ **Bright Idea** ★
Make a whole set of these colorful baubles to trim your tree or to give as gifts!

43

Super Santa

Ho! Ho! Ho! Holidays are happy when this jolly gent arrives!

You Will Need

- red paper
- cardboard tube
- glue
- compass
- pencil
- scissors
- cotton
- thin black cardboard
- gold star sticker
- modeling clay

1 Wrap red paper around a cardboard tube. Glue down the overlapping edge. Set a compass at 2 1/2 inches (6 cm). Draw a circle on red paper and cut it out.

2 Cut the circle in half. Roll one half into a cone. Glue down the overlapping edge and glue the cone onto the tube.

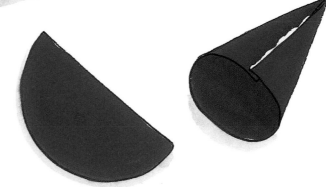

3 Glue a strip of cotton around the bottom of the cone and a small cotton ball at the top of it. Glue a large cotton ball near the middle of the tube for a beard.

44

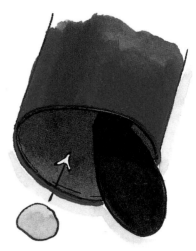

4 Cut a strip of black cardboard and two small black circles. Glue the strip around the tube to make a belt. Glue on the circles for eyes. Add a star sticker for a belt buckle.

5 Cut two feet out of black cardboard. Glue them inside the bottom of the tube. Stick a wad of modeling clay inside the tube for balance.

★ **Bright Idea** ★
Use smaller tubes to make green elves. Instead of cotton beards, give them pointy paper ears.

Kwanzaa Beads

Red, green, and black are Kwanzaa colors. Celebrate this special African holiday by wearing these Kwanzaa-colored beads.

You Will Need
- markers
- paper
- pencil
- ruler
- scissors
- glue stick
- string or cord

1   Use red, green, and black markers to cover a sheet of paper with swirls of color.

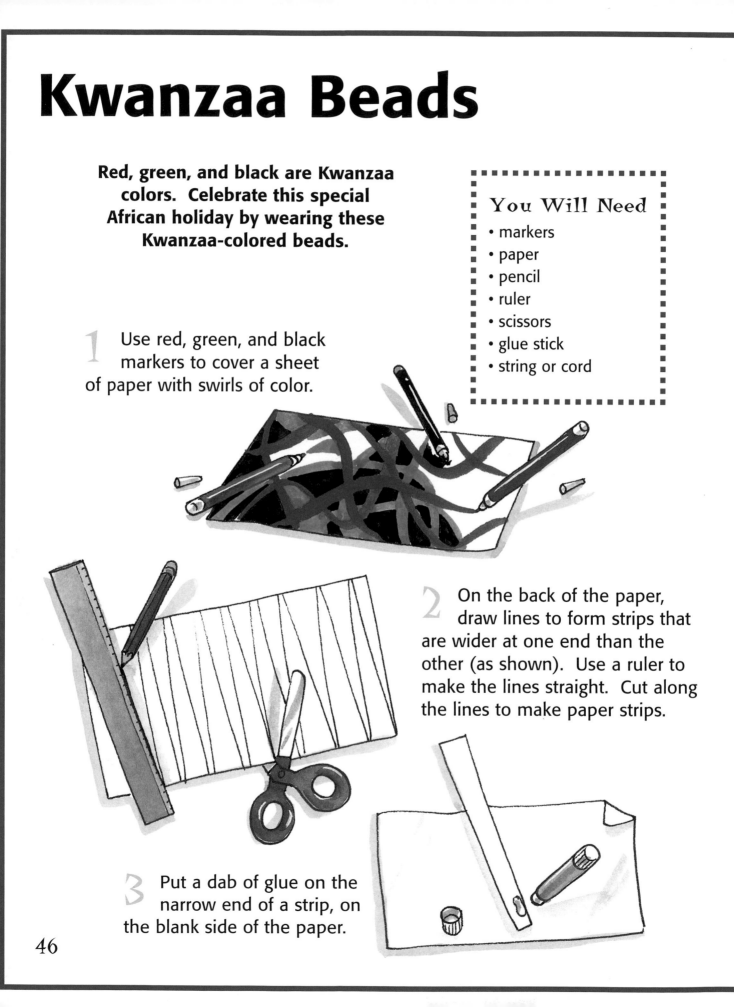

2   On the back of the paper, draw lines to form strips that are wider at one end than the other (as shown). Use a ruler to make the lines straight. Cut along the lines to make paper strips.

3   Put a dab of glue on the narrow end of a strip, on the blank side of the paper.

4   Lay the wide end of the strip over a pencil. Turn the pencil to roll up the strip. Press the glued end down firmly.

★ Bright Idea ★

For more variety, make smaller beads from strips of colored paper that are the same width at both ends.

5   Slide the bead off of the pencil and make some more. Thread the beads onto a long piece of string or cord. Tie the ends of the string together to make a necklace.

Glossary

bauble: a small, showy ornament or trinket.

compass: a tool for drawing circles which has two arms, one with a sharp point and one that holds a pencil.

cone: a shape that has a circular base and curving sides that come to a point at the top.

dowel: a thin, round, smooth stick of wood.

fretsaw: a fine-toothed saw with a narrow blade that is often used to cut curved outlines.

knead: to press and squeeze with the hands, over and over.

matzo: bread traditionally eaten during Passover that is baked thin, crisp, and flat with no yeast to make it rise.

overlapping: lying over the top of something and partly covering it.

pinking shears: scissors with **V**-shaped notches in the blades that leave a zigzag edge as they cut through material.

skewer: a pointed stick made of wood or metal, which is used to hold meat together while the meat is roasting.

varnish: a sticky, paintlike substance spread over a surface to give it a hard finish and a shiny appearance.

wreath: a ring of branches, flowers, or leaves that are twisted or woven together to wear on the head or to hang as a decoration.

More Craft Books by Gareth Stevens

Costume Crafts. Worldwide Crafts (series). Iain MacLeod-Brudenell

Crafty Masks. Crafty Kids (series). Thomasina Smith

Festival Crafts. Worldwide Crafts (series). Chris Deshpande

The Kids' Multicultural Art Book. Williamson Kids Can!® (series). Alexandra M. Terzian

Index

antlers 40-41
April Fool's Day 4, 20
beads 18, 19, 46-47
candle shades 28-29
cardboard tubes 8, 9, 30, 31, 44, 45
Chinese New Year 4, 8
Christmas 5, 36-45
clay 30, 31, 34, 35, 44, 45
cotton 18, 19, 44, 45
cups 6, 7, 8, 26, 27
dragons 8-9
dreidels 34-35

Easter 4, 16-19
egg cartons 8, 18, 19, 26
eggs 16-17
fabric 8, 9, 22, 23
felt 8, 9, 14, 40
flowers 22-23
Halloween 5, 24-29
Hanukkah 5, 34-37
harvest festivals 5, 32-33
hearts 10-13
jumping jacks 20-21
Kwanzaa 5, 46-47

masks 24-25
May Day 5, 22-23

napkin holders 30-31
New Year 4, 6
noisemakers 6-7
painting 8, 16, 17, 28, 35, 36
paper plates 24, 38
Passover 4, 14-15
pipe cleaners 6, 18, 19, 26, 27
pockets 14-15
printing 32-33
pumpkins 24-25

ribbon 12, 13, 20, 21, 36, 37, 40, 41, 42, 43

sequins 14, 15, 42, 43
sewing 15, 22
spiders 26-27
stamps 32-33
stars 36-37, 44, 45
straws 20, 21
Thanksgiving 5, 30-31
turkeys 30-31
Valentine's Day 4, 10-13
wreaths 38-39